Utopian Socialism

Written by

D.B. Taylor

Section I – "The Basis of Utopian Socialism"

Utopian Socialism, these words have the meaning to bring upon the great creation of a glorious society. A society built upon the idea of equality with the firm control of what happens by the people. By dissolving national boarders and by dissolving the heads of all nations and states. In the formation of a single collective to govern the masses. A government forged by the people and in this the true workers state can be formed. No more will we have only one nation in charge but an entire society destined in offering a better life for all those that except it. The chance to create a universal education system, universal healthcare system, and the structure for a better life with universal housing. These systems will be the backbone in forming a stronger relation with the masses. No one will be without and no one will

D.B. Taylor

profit from it.

For this society will be one without corruption, without class separation, and without borders. For the creation of a society is built upon the pillars of educating its citizens. So with the current stance by the Western super powers is to remove funding from the educational system and adding it to the current war profiteering brute force of racial extermination that goes by the name of terrorism. For one has to think who truly created the terrorist states of the world. For with conflict comes oppression which in return slowly creates a nation of followers. A nation of followers creates the perfect totalitarian police state. Built on fear, hate, profit, and death.

As the masses are being pulled by all angles by those who want nothing more to garner support and to line their pockets with what should be given to the masses. The idea that change will come by a single individual is nothing more than a promise from a snake oil salesman that their product truly works. This has been the same formula since the dawn of time. But one can wonder why would the masses

D.B. Taylor

buy into this tried and failed approach? The basis of this is because the masses are truly thoughtless and want to be governed by someone they can relate too. But alas this is only leading them to their bleak deaths. For it has brought nothing but war's built upon lies and creating a society dependent on its elected officials to take care of them. But one must understand that nothing comes free and one must also wonder what the price for this truly is. For as long as the current Government is in power nothing will change.

With this common knowledge within every corner of the working class and even within the halls of Government. We must understand that our current leaders know that within a blink of an eye this current society can change without a second thought and it scares them. By any means necessary change will arrive and who's to say when it will be due. Though many still believe that change for the better will appear through democratic means, which leads one to consider that democratic means is nothing more than a horse and pony show. Where the one person that better

D.B. Taylor

protects the ideology of the corporations and special interest groups will be crowned the victor. With this angle covered by the infinite amount of capital they have at their disposal. The only other means of change for the greater good of the people is through full out revolution.

Thought the masses may linger on this thought as a path not to be treading upon for the fear of being labeled a Terrorist. One also must put into consideration that the founding of their very nation was done through such means to liberate themselves from the hands of their oppressors. With the nations that freed themselves in this fashion now call groups who want change for the greater good of the people and to free themselves from the chains of oppression is truly laughable. The word Terrorist can be used for anyone who doesn't think the same way as the state governs.

As they are now following the same blue print of their former oppressors, they hope to create a state of fear and ignorance. By building an idea of us versus them. One must put into thought of the once mighty empires that ruled

D.B. Taylor

over the masses. They create the idea of fearing the enemy because of their difference in beliefs. This can be seen within today's world. The basis of this is to create a nation of ignorance. For the very basis of continuing a war for profit. How many must die at the hands of such venomous leaders? How many more must fall to the wayside and do nothing when hate is used as a weapon? Though they preach for freedom and democracy they only wish to accomplish more wealth at the cost of human life. When has society evolved to the point where someone's life is worthless compared to the value of natural resources. For this society though claims that they are fighting for the greater good and have an apparent God on their side. While all along worshipping the mighty dollar secretly more than their spiritual creator. This double standard has created the sense that they can do no wrong without any repercussions.

But how long will this trend last? Some think it'll continue till the end of life on this planet. As some believe that their time has come to an end. For with the current economic state of many

D.B. Taylor

first world nations who have seen the error of their ways.

The masses must no longer believe in these self-appointed God's of government. That the lies they have been telling aren't fooling anyone. No more will those innocent people that spill their blood for the profiteers. No more will wars be fought for resources on the backs of lies. When will the senselessness of our faith in the current governments survive?

The time has arrived; the call for a full scale global revolution has come to the ears of everyone who desires change for the greater good. To make corruption within government a thing of the past. For wars with no meaning and unjust to never happen again. We must stand together not as several nations but as one group. A group under the banner of Utopian Socialism. For within this idea brings forth the idea of equality, of peace, where everyone will be employed, no one will go hungry, and be given an equal chance for an education and healthcare. No more will there be those who can't move forward on the basis of because they can't afford it.

D.B. Taylor

As time slowly fades away, we are stepping closer to the realization that our once powerful government is now nothing more than a decrypted shell. Withered away and soon on death's door.

For any nation that appears to be powerful and unstoppable always has the weakest infrastructure. With this the fear of an imperial dragon sitting perched on a tower ready for a fight will be defeated by a sizeable army. For with this image of being undefeated by the forces of an enemy nation. How will any government's armies be able to fire upon their citizens? Simple the majority of them will be unable too. Under the simple code of humanity, humanity for the common citizen. For no matter how large the army when it comes to an uprising of the masses subconsciously they are aware of the dyer scenario that they are a part of.

A new war is slowly brewing, not one over resources, or one built upon a lie. But a war built upon the wave of change that many are seeing has to happen for a truly glorious society to be constructed. This construction will be the largest within the world. Putting

D.B. Taylor

aside personnel beliefs in religion and culture and working together in the construction of a new world built upon the principles of Utopian Socialism.

The formation of the new Utopian Socialist Government will be built without a single individual in charge. But will be established with a council. A council for every aspect of life from production, to the production and harvesting of natural resources. To that of education and the health sector. These councils will be built by the finest minds in their fields. Everyone will have a voice and can participate in said councils as equals.

Everyone will be employed and everyone will be in charge of shaping the political and production aspect of society. A world built with no titles, no financial gain in any way, and no separation of class.

A world built upon these principles will never need to deal with the diseases created by greed. All third world nations will be repaired and

D.B. Taylor

returned to their former first world status. The global banks will seize to exist. No more will there be a need for currency of any kind. But everyone will be paid by what they need to survive "food, utilities, transportation, clothes, and a home". With the extinction of the monetary system everyone will be on the same level, working together as one, and existing as one.

The creation of a Universal Education System will benefit the entire populous. Those who were turned down for the chance of an education or those who didn't have the opportunity will finally have the chance. For a society that is open to the chance for educating the masses will be truly gifted for the second generation. Imagine the great leaps and bounds society will make when the focus isn't on war and greed. But upon the very grasp of bettering society as a whole.

A world where ignorance is a thing of the past and where education is key. For educating the masses for a better tomorrow is more awarding than anything desired.

D.B. Taylor

An example in which this is visible is within the supposed super power of the west "The United State of America". A society built upon slavery and when that was found to be unpopular decided to be for democracy and freedom. But fails where other nations rise. When it comes to education we see this supposed self-appointed powerful nation. Education is nothing more than a branch that can be trimmed for everything it is worth. With this we see that the masses are highly uneducated and ignorant at anything that seems foreign to them. This can be made more clearer as they are repeating the isolationism of the fallen kingdoms that crumbled at the hands of the social uprising's in the east that were funded by those who wanted a foot in the door for a chance to make an alliance for underpriced resources.

The supposed enemy of this super power is a nation that oppresses its people. That isn't a democracy and doesn't allow freedom of speech. For a time being this was the thought of Communism. But with Communism being the main enemy of the supposed west. The

D.B. Taylor

common enemy was that of Russia. But in this day and age we see that the greatest life support of the supposed "United States" that prides itself on supporting liberty and freedom needing a helping hand from a nation such as China. Though one may think that this is truly a fine example of western hypocrisy. But this is just one of the many examples on why this revolution must happen. To put an end towards those nations that self-appoint themselves as the saviors of liberty and freedom for all, must be abolished, and made only that of a footnote in the history of failed empires.

Another example of a system that never was destined to approve the world is that of the "United Nations". This supposed form of global politics was supposed to be the force to stop another world war from taking place and to help better the lives of all people's through discussion rather than war. But we see that this not effective in any way possible. As the "United Nations" hasn't helped in any matter globally.

This also can be made apparent that the "United Nations" is nothing more

D.B. Taylor

than a bloated symbol of what is wrong with the world today.

This symbol of global power is a symbol of the old world. For now we must focus on how we as a people must preserve the future for all.

For the days leading up to the beginning of the social crusades will be a path built upon the backs of the working class. The idea of all people being created equal is something that we would like to believe. But one who looks back in history can see that when that term is used, it is being used to blind the masses for equality has never been truly practiced within our society. For as long as there is class structure and those who sit upon their thrones made from the bones of those that they have exploited. The word equality has no meaning.

As the days leading up for revolution will begin small. An event has to happen within a nation for the seed of revolution to grow and blossom into the flower of Utopian Socialism. Either in

D.B. Taylor

the taking of the rights of its citizens or by the means of economic depression. For those who must work to survive will lose everything within a short matter of time. These people will be left out in the streets to wither away and die. These victims of a poisoned system will be the first to realize the errors of their way. For these people must have a voice, a voice calling to them to not allow those with power to push them to the wayside. These people will be the back bone of the revolution.

We can see the current enslavement of the masses in the form of the so called mighty Union. This creation of benefitting and protecting the common worker is nothing more than a wolf in sheep's clothing. Used in keeping the masses at bay by allowing them to think that they are truly protected by the means of the head of corporations. This too can be seen as nothing more than a pawn, a pawn to keep the people at bay. For it is easy to allow the masses to think that they are protected by their supposed rights. The creation of any union is to simply hold back the cries of the masses. These unions are nothing

D.B. Taylor

more than a middle man for corruption.

It is easy to keep the masses at bay
with the creation of an organization
that claims it is to protect the
workers. The same can be said for the
banking system trying to help the masses
in allowing them to live the dream of
having a family and owning their home.
Though much can be said within the
protection of the rights of the workers.
Shorter working days, benefits, etc. But
these ideas and beliefs are just a small
portion of what can be accomplished.
These table scraps from the wealthy
business owners are used as a weapon. A
weapon to keep the masses from stepping
out of line and laying claim to more.
For the existence of a union is to keep
the masses from standing up and laying
claim for the existence of a socialist
society.

As with every country that's in bed
with capitalism and with every President
of every company that profits more than
any third world nation corruption is
always key to their success. The human
factor is slowly replaced with the
cancer of profit. For the creation of
Union's have been nothing more than the

D.B. Taylor

bullpen of corruption. As within the creation of Utopian Socialism the basis and formation of Union's must be erased from the working platform of all people's. Every reminder of corruption and marker of enslavement must be phased out within a span of five years. For the enlightenment of the workers matters more than profits and control. These old reminders from the days of slavery must not be held on to with the white gloves of the bankers. Full out violent means should be taken. No more will the self-appointed rulers over society will be sitting back and watching the chaos unfold for others to deal with. We shall take it to their doorsteps and finally vanquish them in the formation of a truly successful society that will stand the test of time and bring forth the means of equality. This society will be a marker of the great achievements of the human race. Under the banner of Utopian Socialism. The creation of a new world will stand for a better world, the people will benefit from all the glorious fruits from this tree. But first the masses must know what it means to sacrifice for within the creation of any truly great society the masses must

D.B. Taylor

sacrifice. A collection of people's must be gathered and the use of carnal force must be used in this formation. Within history we see that all truly strong nations have gone through this metamorphous. The metamorphous will not be one through peace but through full scale revolution. The idea of revolution fills the rulers of the old world with fear, fear of change, the fear that they will lose everything that they stole from the people. Once the spark has been lite and the people march forward towards the capital then we are shown the true colors of these self-appointed rulers of the nation. For the fight must move forward and never stop for a moment, stopping will only bring about the question of doubt, doubt is the enemy in any movement of a grand scale. The people must be ready, the nation must be ready, and the time must be now.

With the dismantling of the financial districts of the old world, the new world must be built upon the elimination of the finical institutes. By not the means of democracy but through erasing them all together. As the world has stopped in mid change and the populous

D.B. Taylor

has increased the cry for change is beginning to echo louder and louder. Once the financial institutes have been erased then are we as a people are truly able to move forward towards the path of peace. For there will be no more fear of losing everything, the basis of fear of never knowing what will happen to one's family if the economy collapses once again.

The perfect weapon in holding the people back has to be that of the economy. For the economy is faceless and has no pulse but yields the power of an old King. A King that can wipe out an entire social class. It can give support to a Dictator or give way in erasing an entire people from existence. It can back a war or hold a nation in the grip of depression. This faith in a non-existent being is the face of a new religion that has replaced those of the old world. Faith in capital and the belief that it can heal all those that accept it is truly pathetic. Since when have we as a species have given in to these religious practices. Why have we allowed them to hold us back from our full potential? Question's like these

D.B. Taylor

must be answered by any means necessary. For it is our time to take a stand against the politics of greed. Once the dragon of greed has been slayed and those who harness it's ever destructive power, then are we truly free from the realization that they have no power. That they have enslaved the human race for generations with the idea that they are truly able to do us harm. But all along have been bluffing from the beginning. Once we abolish the use of currency and the process to create money from thin air and allow this money to have some sort of value. Then are we truly free.

One can be sure that the fight for liberty, of all peoples from all corners of the world will arrive. The streets must be marched upon to victory. For the governments of all nations no matter how powerful they claim to be are built upon a foundation of sand. For within any given time a government can crumble into ruin. The creation of a provisional government in replacing the former government through means of democratic formation is that of a shadow of its former self under the disguise of

D.B. Taylor

change. A nation with its current government in the ash heap of history will be powerless for exacting complete change in protecting the methods of the previous government. The conflict between politician and military commander will soon be witnessed. The politician will soon realize that no amount of empty promises will grant them the power they once had. For the military will do anything to restore the peace and stability of the government, they are seen as the last defense towards the very existence of the nation. That they will do anything to defend the government at any cost. But one must look towards the human factor of the military. For how many of its troops will be openly alright with firing upon the citizens? The answer lies within the human element of the troops. For anyone can claim to take the life of another in self-defense of one's self and for the stability of the nation they sworn to protect. The military is the final call for defense in this matter for those in charge are aware that within a short period of time the military would either collapse at the hands of the masses or join in the fight

D.B. Taylor

for the ever glorious cause to benefit their own survival.

With this the fear of the old reigning empires of the supposed world will soon discover that their existence is on borrowed time and make the decision to either flee or attempt to take back what they believe is rightfully theirs. Or allow them to be captured in the hopes of negotiating their surrender. One must be prepared to not show any humanity as for they will pray upon this weakness to cloud the judgment of their captures and attempt to take back what they think is their duty. Insulting the intelligence of the masses by thinking that they can't govern themselves, like that of a parent who feels the need to rule over the child's life in a belief that they aren't capable of making their own decisions.

For it is the duty of every Socialist to take a stand, to arm themselves, and to slay the dragon of oppression no matter what form it tries to disguise it's self with.

D.B. Taylor

The Utopian Socialist movement must be built as soon as the government has fallen. Though Utopian Socialism is to create a society with not a single government in charge. The construction period will take a few years to create. The presence of a single government will exist for the time being until the creation of the People's Councils are put into place. This will govern the production of all forms of goods manufactured or grown.

Within this creation of manufactured goods and that within the agricultural sector. The people will be given the items needed to exist and will be given food to feed their families. The masses will not need to wait in lines for hours at a time to retrieve such items but will be delivered to their doorstep. This will be assured that they are truly an important part in the machine of Utopian Socialism. For whatever path is required to create a society such as this, rewarding the masses is a must in a grand jester for those who have worked for it.

As we must stand together against the regime of the old world, we must

D.B. Taylor

remember that surrender is never an option. Nor is it the basis of any successful society. The repercussions will set back the movement of full scale global revolution back hundreds of years.

For with every aspect of production must be utilized to its full potential. The era of the welfare state has come to its end. No more will the masses hold out their hands for support from the government. For this is a leash around the necks of all those entrapped in the snare of capitalism.

The time has arrived for all peoples who are tired of the ways of the old world. Utopian Socialism has arrived and with it the human populous can voyage forward in the creation of a truly wonderful society. That's boundaries are unlimited and will shuttle forth a new age in evolution.

D.B. Taylor

Section II – "The Foundation of a new Planned Economy under Utopian Socialism

"Throughout the existence of human development and through the development of the social structure, came forth the many forms of economic development. From the "Hunter Gatherer Societies from the very beginning of mankind's existence. All the way to Feudalism and the establishment hierarchy that brought upon Lords and Peasants. Which in turn lead way to the evolution of a class structure and lay the foundations towards the path of both the ideologies of Communism and Capitalism."

Utopian Socialism, the basis of what we all strive to create. A world built upon the ideas of Socialism, built upon the platform of equality, and that of a Planned Economy. For its creation can happen at any given time and in any given country. For it could be started

D.B. Taylor

within a small town, to a city, or in a Province or State. For its creation will be that of equality and with it the shell of Capitalism will crumble back into the ash heap of human evolution.

For those that doubt the platform which is Utopian Socialism one can simply look to the past at former society's that took the step forward and attempted to prove to the world that Capitalism isn't the only path we can take.

For the transformation from a Capitalist society over to Utopian Socialism is one that is quite difficult but never the less it is possible. For the transfer of private property will be handed out equally to those in need. No more will the masses have to pay the vast amount of interest for residence with an over inflated price tag. That almost is double what it cost to build the house in the first place. Those who are within a life time of never being able to afford it will have what the supposed masters of society claim is the dream of independence.

A dream built upon lies is just that,

D.B. Taylor

a lie. For the idea of living a dream of independence in owning one's own home is the formation of the ever eternal rat race. For in the end once it is paid off you must still pay property tax. So even though one has accomplished this supposed dream, one is never truly free of paying for it. Within the existence of this society we find that no matter what path one takes in bettering themselves for the greater good, we see that they still end up at the same finishing line. Rich or poor at the end we all end up in the same place. So this idea of hard working and trying to accomplish the dream of capitalism ends up with an entire generation not wanting a better life for the next. This can be certainly seen within the recent health crisis of this generation, a generation built upon gelutney, genetically manufactured food, additives, chemicals, and addiction.

The previous generation knew that and even with this knowledge turned their backs on the current generation in order of making a vast profit. Lower quality foods and the easiness of preparing a simple meal at a push of a button have

D.B. Taylor

significantly dealt a slow blow to the masses. This has brought life expectance to not surpass that of the previous generation. This lays claim to the idea that those in charge of every aspect of human existence in the guise of government and those sitting upon their thrones of ivory in their board rooms.

For this act against the current generation is seen as the biggest act of genocide on such a scale that everyone will be affected in one way or another. Causing such a heavy burden on the current uncertain medical sector. This could also be seen as a way to change the current socialist medical system into the disgusting form known as the private medical sector. That when the time has arrived and it will. The medical sector will collapse and then the supposed saviors of humanity will claim that it is the people's fault and that the system must be accommodated at best to help those in need. This will create another sector that will pray upon those without the means of affording healthcare. In it we will see the biggest form of extortion, the basis that no generation has ever seen before.

D.B. Taylor

If the medical sector is allowed to become privatized than we will see the bound between government and corporation form stronger than ever. They will decide who will live and who will die. They will decide who will be allowed for treatment and who those will parish.

In other sectors of government this is made apparent from within the military sector. Corporations who have no loyalty for their nation or the people but to those who are the highest bidder. For the current global conquests between nations, freedom fighters, and between other groups all are carrying the same weapons as those soldiers from the supposed super powers. The question could be asked. How did they acquire these weapons? And the answer is quite simple from representatives of said weapons manufacturing companies. Now who is to say when or how they were purchased but the fact of the matter is that when you begin leasing out contracts in the formation of healthcare, weapons manufacturing, the agricultural sector, and every other sector that is supposed to benefit the people to corporations and banks that

D.B. Taylor

hold no loyalty to the nation that they are founded in. Than why must we sit and do nothing while these modern day warlords govern over our very existence. How long will it be until they decide that half the human populous isn't needed and they just decide to enact a genocide policy to better benefit them?

For the time of being languid is over. How long will it be until a loved one is lost? How long until the chemicals in our very foods begin to dwindle the ones we love with decease? How long will it be till the movement takes a stand and forwards through to the den of the beast? It will happen within the next few years. As people begin to see the reason to why corporations have acted the way they had.

One may say that the government is truly at fault for it has handed over the reins of production over to the private sect. But that cannot be put into aspect for our elected officials have become lazy over the years, by allowing the private sect access to every aspect of life on such a global scale the vision of profit is hypnotic

D.B. Taylor

to those with in its grasp. For the governments of the world are guilty for allowing such a takeover of humanity in being formed. For this allows products that aren't safe for human consumption being packages and sold overseas to nations that are more lenient to corporations and have lower standards for its citizens.

With this the masses of those countries will become victims, these victims will be angry, angry at their supposed government that's job is to protect them from an outside threat. But we can see that their anger will fall upon the empty theatre of the United Nations. For the lives of those in developing nations have no value over those in nations of the first world. Why? Because money is to be made of it.

Once you stop and realize that everyone's life has a price and that those in the first world are deemed more valuable than those from a developing nation.

Who is guilty in allowing such crimes to unfurl? Is it the Capitalist? Or, maybe the Government? Or are the people,

D.B. Taylor

who haven't been more active in how the marriage between government and the corporations?

All are guilty parties in one way or another, not only one can be blamed or only one can lay blame. The blame falls upon everyone. But the difference between the three is that two are profiting off it and not being effected by their actions. As the masses are being subjected by profiteering, been experimented on in one way or another by genetically modified foods, chemicals in the water, and in the air. Or sent off to fight for a cause just so that a foothold can be made in acquiring natural resources.

Another form of manipulating the masses is that of the advertising sect. These masters of selling snake oil to the masses by promoting a healthy and clean lifestyle by using their products can be plainly seen. As this weapon of the corporations takes a product and makes one feel as if their life would be complete and that they can live like those in the one percent. Also by poisoning the minds of the people by thinking that they will look better than

D.B. Taylor

they do. Playing on the insecurities of the many allows them to churn a profit that will allow them to continue for years.

This is seen more in the field of the housing market and luxury aspect of our poisoned capitalist society. The idea that one having a large home, a wonderful luxury automobile, and other useless objects that allow many to believe that one has acquired success is truly repulsive. This is the basis of another trick by those in the banking sect and corporate sect. A marriage seen ever so clearer in recent years. Believed to be only an affair and that the real marriage was between Country and the Banking System. This belief was quickly shattered by the event leading up to and after the economic collapse of 2008. For who profited off the idea of selling the idea of success? The basis of the dream of a first world nation. For anyone no matter how much they make or what they do for a living. The banking sect saw this as an easy opportunity in accumulating more wealth based on the principles of interest.

The corporate sect sold the idea of

D.B. Taylor

what success is and sold it to those just beneath the middle class. Which in turn made those in the middle class think that they too can have everything that those in the wealthy category have, but without having to work for it? This in turn created more revenue for the corporate sect which in turn created more revenue for the banking sect. As the majority of the people they allowed to live the dream of the elite were working meaningless jobs and had no way in ever affording to fully payoff what they have purchased. Within turn allowed the banking sect to accumulate a vast fortune off the interest of the millions who had fallen for the scheme.

Not wanting to lose everything they had acquired has brought upon an attempt in the creation of locking those who have fallen victim to greed and the also signed their lives away in the hopes that they can one day be among those in the one percent. This attempt can be said that they wanted to create a generation forever in debt and yes it is true. But that wasn't the case, with the vast amounts of debt those built up by trying to attempt the lifestyle that

D.B. Taylor

they ever so wanted to emulate. Brought upon the greatest enemy of any capitalist nation; financial ruin. Not only for countries but in the very den of the beast.

For if it wasn't for the economic collapse of 2008, who's to say what could have happened? A generation forever in debt? With no hope of ever being free; No one is certain as the economic collapse brought to the fore front the truth. That the governments of the world were no longer in any form of power. That the banking sect had held the world hostage in exchange for whatever amount they requested. The final nail in the coffin was when it was given to them. For at the fore front of leadership over humanity and of nations isn't that of a single government but that of those in the board rooms in the corporate sect and of the banking sect.

Who is to say what will happen in the next ten years or so? Who is to say it won't get any worse? One thing is for certain that nothing will happen for the greater good with the supposed true leaders of the world at the helm.

D.B. Taylor

With Capitalism we have seen the creation of powerful corporations. With Capitalism we have seen innovations be made and destroyed by those who wanted to create a better world. By the notion that profit couldn't be made.

One can find many more examples throughout history but these were just a few taken in recent years. For the economic theory of Capitalism has out lived its usefulness and must be changed for the greater good. For it is the end of the free market economy and the dawn of a new planned economy. For a nation built upon the principles of Capitalism can slowly be converted into a Socialist society. Though the path of change will take some time to fully evolve into the full people's economy.

The basis for the transformation into a Planned Economy will happen within the forming of several councils. As the means of it include "planning, balance of materials, quotas, rationing, technical coefficients, budgetary controls with limits, price and wage control, and with other techniques in the process of production within the limits of the Planned Economy. This can

D.B. Taylor

also benefit the means of labor within it for it will allow the many to have employment.

As stated previously the Planned Economic structure will need to be slowly implemented through a period of five years. To allow the formation of councils which will vote on what must be produced for the year. This will also be the final step in the process of planning for the economy.

The first step will be that of "I. Collectivization of data, this will be effective in finding out what the people need. Through setting up input centers around the many cities and in rural areas, by collecting this data on the needs are, the Council's will have a better grasp on what needs to be done to keep the people happy. Which in turn will keep production at an ever rising pace. This alone will also help plan for what resources will be needed the following year if the trend for a certain item is in such high demand".

The second step will be that of Cybernetics. "II. The idea behind Cybernetics is that the usage of

D.B. Taylor

computers to coordinate production. This was used by the Economist Oskar Lange. For by using computers for this process we can better keep track and predict the growth of production in the means of what resources are readily available at the time. Even through economic hardship on a global scale or that a certain resource has become hard to retrieve. The Cybernetics system can help in predicting what is needed the most over what isn't. For with todays technological means this can be accomplished on such a grand scale. This practice has been put to use by many nations before and to present day. This prevents the production of useless goods that aren't needed and by producing such useless products creates a strain on the vault of resources which could be used in others means, to better society rather than be squandered away".

Than once that's complete we move on to the third and finally step. "III. The Planning Committee, for with gathering the input from the masses and the inputting of such information in the Cybernetics system to best determine what should be produced with the idea of

D.B. Taylor

waste of such resources in the front of one's minds. The Planning Committee will go over all the data collected and through a series of democratic voting will best determine what will and won't be produced. This system will not affect the medical sect, educational sect, and the housing sect. But will affect the production of certain items within the housing sect such as luxurious produced goods." *Within the agricultural sect the same system will be put into place but a separate committee will be setup for it.*

This formation of collecting data, analyzing the data, and finally voting on it. Is the tier system of the economic system. This will better benefit the means of the masses being with what they will need to survive. Also through this matter no one will be without, though one must tread carefully as there are many distractions which can cause those to turn off the path of the Planned Economy.

The cancerous decay brought upon the monetary system will always be lurking its ugly head around the corner, waiting for the people's economy to lower its

D.B. Taylor

guard and then strike with vengeance in a desperate act to not allow society to lose sight of the power that comes with the monetary system. The cancer known as money has brought down such mighty empires throughout history. The means of money creates a system of inequality for all. Once the abolishment of the monetary system is in effect than can the system truly flourish for the greater good. But for as long as it still breathes the greatest threat will still lurk, the evil of greed. For money will pollute the minds of those working in the system, it will cloud one's judgment from producing what one needs and in return will slowly choke the life out of the economy in the means of an "Underground Economy". This form of an economy that is backed with money will slowly be the venom in stealing the life from the Planned Economy. For the "Underground Economy" is built upon the system of supply and demand, if one were to purchase a car they would have to pay an inflated price for the model and options. This can also be with the natural resources such as fossil fuels or with food. This in turn will slowly destroy the very heart of the Planned

D.B. Taylor

Economy. This will create a massive inflation in produced goods that are not purchased by the masses do to the fact that they purchased them through other means. This in return will slowly build a barrier between the masses, a barrier built on the amount of money collected by such dealings.

Such crimes against the masses must be better monitored for even in today's world the existence of the "Underground Economy" exists and will do whatever it takes to undermine any economic system it wishes. For even in a Capitalist System, the basis of such an economy also damages it's economy, by purchasing something at a lower price than off the store shelves will slowly collapse it's mode of production. Within the entertainment industry this is made more visible by piracy. One can simply stop piracy from happening; one can stop, push a button and simply make it disappear. With that said the arms of the "Underground Economy" has a grasp they will stretch for infinity. Where ever a profit is to be made than it will stop at nothing to try and collect what it can.

D.B. Taylor

Monitoring of such activities must be used to its full extent. By any means necessary such as "the government, police, military, and banks". Such crimes against the economic system of the masses must be dealt with a harsh penalty to best suit the crime committed. Though the enemy of a "Planned Economy" is that of the "Underground Economy". One must take note that the committees must never discuss or do business with those in military, business sect, and other individuals who may benefit from the production of any produced goods. For the threat of bribery and financial gain will prove to favor what a small handful of those require, either for their own financial gain or to sell for an increased profit on the global market. This in turn will weaken the foundation of the economy.

Those who are appointed to govern on such committee's to better monitor and vote on production for the country. Will be allowed only to serve two terms, while each term is only that of a two year span. To also prevent those becoming too comfortable in their

D.B. Taylor

positions and to prevent corruption from accruing. Audit's within the committee's will also take place every two years to also prevent corruption from taking place too ensure that the committees are doing what they can to benefit the society.

For such resources must not surpass the economic planning stage, if it is needed for the production of goods, then it will be used for such manufactured good. It must not be taken from the production line and used in other areas of production. This will create a break in the chain of the economy. This will also weaken faith within the Planned Economy and will slowly move towards the complete disintegration of the economy.

Though if a Planned Economy takes place in North America with its vast amounts of resources or in Europe today the results of the Planned Economy will be more successful than in previous years. This can be truly a great feet for their will be no massive shortages of raw materials.

For the creation of a Planned Economy in this and age will better

D.B. Taylor

benefit the future of society. One can imagine the vast wastage of resources due to over producing of several items that aren't sold. Thus creating a surplus in which cause the economy and corporations to lose profits. This is the reason why Capitalism doesn't work in today's society. As it wastes much needed natural resources and cause a surplus which in doubt weakens the economy. The true weapon of any economic system is that of a surplus, the surplus is a disease which eats away at the market.

Such resources can be better used in the beneficial matter of helping the entire world. The waste and labor put in such useless items can be better harnessed in the creation of a better world. One has to wonder with all the time put into making products that sell poorly or don't sell at all what is the true outcome of this venture into Capital? With the mode of production transferred from the west and into a country such as China, the idea of Capitalism being the mecca of power is seen but at the price of modern day slavery. The term slavery is a taboo in

D.B. Taylor

of itself. Where a society built upon slavery is a society destined to failure one has to wonder how can modern day slavery survive in this day and age? The answer is simpler than one can imagine.

For a society built on Capitalism needs to manufacture goods at a low cost, that includes the cost of materials, the cost of labor, the cost of manufacturing, and the cost of shipping to the numerous retail stores around the world. With the idea that the less spent on the product the more they will charge which in turn equals more profit. So with this most of the high end companies will move their manufacturing plants into countries that have low to no safety laws and rights for their employees. As the unions took over protecting the rights of the workers that fall under their blanket of protection with the laws governed by the government. The cost for manufacturing such goods such as "Computers, Automobiles, Clothes, Luxury items, etc etc." Are all sent overseas to a nation for in turn will enslave its masses in exchange for vast amounts of financial gain. This creates a sense of laziness

D.B. Taylor

in the working class in such western nations such as the United States and others who are angry at the transition that their country has taken but in some way still support it by buying the products they could have made themselves which in turn would have employed them. Though some industries which practice this to its fullest extent will still produce some form of the product such as can be seen in the automotive sect. This creates the image that they still care but in all realism is just a marketing gimmick that show's that they still somewhat care about those at home.

As the cost of paying labor is increasingly lower now and with the massive payments made to the country of China. We begin to see the true face of Capitalism, the face of oppression in which those who built the products have to face "Low wages, no health care, no maternity leave, no pension, and no rights". Some of the biggest companies in North America have approved of this hard treatment of the workers who are practically modern day slaves. Though they will deny this to the very end. The truly repulsive matter is that everybody

D.B. Taylor

knows this, everybody knows about the horrid conditions and limited rights those who produce the goods they buy, and yet they can careless. The humanity has been sucked out of modern day civilization.

People living in squalor conditions with hardly any running water, little for food to feed their families, and nothing to show for it except for being able to barely survive. This in turn will create the next generation of modern day slaves, working day in and day out trying to survive. But this can only last for so long. The workers can only be pushed long enough until they demand a change in the way things are being ran. This has happened once before in China, where the workers who wanted a raise increase in wages. They were tired of being ignored and planned on a mass suicide to prove their point. In return they stopped production for a bit, which meant that the big corporations such as Microsoft and Apple would have to supposedly try and work with the people in preventing such negative publicity from damaging the image of their products. In exchange to try and make

D.B. Taylor

the matter better in their favor and in an attempt to boost morale, these companies and others gave the workers a raise. Which realistically is only applying a bandage on a massive wound, the problem may be settled for now, but when massive assembly plants in China have to install suicide prevention nets in protecting its work force from killing themselves what does that say about the conditions the workers face every day. Though going on the record and offering them a raise but at what cost, who's to say that they aren't revoking their basic rights as a punishment. No amount of money given to the workers will ever really benefit them or their families because they are still far below the poverty line as it is. It is easy to point the blame at the corporations for allowing such treatment of its workers and by allowing them to live in worse conditions than that of the beginning of the industrial revolution in England. Such crimes must be met with harsh consequence. The governments of the west should be held at fault as well and the governments of the east. For they all share the same amount of the blame as the corporations.

D.B. Taylor

For allowing to turn their backs on the needs of their own very people. This will create a new conflict, not one that has been seen with this generation.

The next generation will become ever bitter towards the west and Capitalism. This could create a new government bent on the ways and teachings of Maoism. For the wounds of the past dealt by those in the west could create a new cold war.

Though corporate sect and the governments of those nations which allowed such crimes to be committed are to blame the real victims of this new war will be that of the children. The next generation, they will have to deal with the cleanup of the environment, an environment left on life support. One could think that the effects of the previous generation led to the mighty advances in technology and vast production which spread across the world like a condor stretching its wings can be taken as a good example of how far we have come along. But in realistic views we haven't moved forward but instead have taken ten steps back. For allowing the creation of modern day slavery in

D.B. Taylor

the guise of Capitalism. This will spread forth a new civil war, but on such a grand scale that it could be classified as a planetary war, a war for the creation of equality, the likes the world has never seen before. A full scale class war under the banner of Utopian Socialism. This sounds like the talk of a mad man, but think about it in terms of the repercussions of greed.

Like the war of Independence in the United States, or the Civil War, or the expansion of the West and the mass slaughter of the Native American's. The past has a way of repeating itself and those who are blind and ignorant and think that they can't stop it from continuing it are wrong. For it is easy not to do anything and continue to support it because it works for you, but the cost of it is far greater than anyone could imagine it. The price down the road to repair the damages and destruction caused by those who feast upon wealth and the accumulation of it will be far greater than anyone could for see. Perhaps in the next few decades when the current generation are replaced with their children. Fueled by

D.B. Taylor

frustration of the economic system that allowed them to become enslaved, their hatred of the west and all that it stands for. This will cease production in the east and will force the west to either attempt to produce the goods that they readily had before, or move into another country that cares nothing for its people.

This will be the death of Capitalism. As with every political setup and economic market, change will occur as society moves forward. For it is our need to survive that will change the system and the world.

D.B. Taylor

Section III – "The Principles of Utopian Socialism"

The creation of a Utopian Society is called nothing more than a dream for those who believe in a better world but are afraid of what path it may take. The idea of this is truly a blunt knife trying to pierce a suit of armor. Those who question those who believe in Utopianism, a society built upon equality for all, a better world for those who have nothing but a grim grasp on reality.

For those who talk negatively on the subject are those who wish not for change but for that of the old system to continue on life support for as long as it can. These individuals continue to look back at formal attempts in the creation of a pure socialist state and continue to blind those that know no better with classic fear mongering. For

D.B. Taylor

the path towards the foundation of Utopianism as with the formation of any society, blood is spilled. The fear of this happening now is a prime example of how the current crumbling empires of the old world. With the seed of change comes the arrival of fear, fear of losing what one has gained through the efforts of others.

One has to understand that through change of any kind may it be economic, political, social, etc etc etc. Has always been built upon conflict between the system of old and those who sacrifice for the change to better those who have nothing to gain but the hope of a better world.

The constant bullying by nations that oppose such change must be held in contempt of human evolution. These self-appointed first world nations built upon either revolutionary means or by others means such as through the defeat in war. Change is necessary for society as a whole to move forward, but those who are blinded by wealth and Capitalism are prone to have those who want to move forward by calling them heretic's and in today's world by calling them

D.B. Taylor

terrorists. These people of power, the marriage of mankind and money have laid waste to the human race as a whole.

The need in moving forward is human nature but so is constantly gaining material possessions to reflect how successful one is. This can stem back to the days of Tribalism. When the more one has the more than one individual seems to be more desirable to those who have little to nothing. This is the cancer we find in western civilization and the cancer found in every human being. The need to be loathed for one has and the need to show what one possess is almost in a sense what brings upon the worst in people and in turn will bring ruin to humanity.

Once we are able to free ourselves from this useless human attribute than are we able to move forward. This idea that we can move forward without being attached by the chain of material and financial possessions. This brings fear to those in charge of just a nation but the life force of all nations "The International Banks". Once this has been completed than the next step is the formation of a Utopianist Government.

D.B. Taylor

For this Government will be forged out of the remains of the collapsed monarchs of the old world. The road to its creation is never certain on how the outcome will be of the finished product. For the foundation is written for all those who wish to pander on the idea that is presented to you.

As from any given period of time from the dawn of Tribalism to the Present day marriage between Socialism and Capitalism. That within any time frame of human society it is possible for the formation of a Utopian world. It is not something that we the people have to wait around for a few decades or a millennia but we can begin construction of the principle ideology of Utopianism.

But the only road block on our path of success is the basis that this will never be accomplished by the naysayers who think this is completely unrealistic. This is the same group that over a hundred years ago laughed at the idea of women being seen as equals and having the right to vote. The idea that we can form a new society built upon the basis of a Utopian society may seem alien. But what can be said is that

D.B. Taylor

society is always moving forward and that no idea, no matter how it sounds should be erased from the board of human development without being fully looked at and examined. Imagine how far we can move forward in such a short time once we free ourselves from those who want us, the people to stand still while they take us for everything that we are worth. Like a ship being held in place by an anchor. It holds the ship still but ever being affected by the waves and by any storms that reach the ship.

But as a ship that has an anchor, we as Utopian Socialist's must free ourselves from our supposed anchor of other forms of Socialist's such as the "Communist's" because of the stigma that is associated with them. Even though we have the same common goal the black eye that is associated with them will do more harm than good in our favor. For we must cut ourselves free from them and move onward on our own in the formation of the true Utopian society that we wish to create in the image of peace and love.

All forms of Socialism lead down the path of Communism, but just like any

D.B. Taylor

road travelled there always appears a road block and that road block for us is Communism. Though many worship the idea of Communism the fact of the matter is that it is an idea well tainted in a shadow of oppression and terror. Those who object in the first world do not see the true horror's that it brings to those who live under it. For example the slave labor in China, the crimes under Stalin during his reign in the Soviet Union. These few examples are why Communism will never achieve any form of success within the western world, mainly in the United States and Canada.

Though to keep the people intact many nations have adopted socialist policy's to prevent the masses to seize power in a full scale revolution.

Though many would like to see a full scale global revolution under the banner of a Marxist society which will never come to prevision. We must look to other means of moving forward, Communism is an idea that no one wants to revisit and shouldn't be bothered in practicing again. Though many will say the same with Fascism, though they are still around in full force but under a new

D.B. Taylor

name "Capitalists". We can't help but to turn to the past and wonder what could work for us in our favor. The many Billions of workers who try and attempt to make a living, supporting their loved ones, and trying to move forward in the world.

The idea that the masses who believe in Utopianism are nothing more than those who are living in a dream world is despicable. Those who believe that it will never happen have given up on moving forward. These individuals have given up on the idea that after Communism lye's nothing but the bleak foundation of human existence and that is all. But with Socialism leads to Communism which in turn leads to Utopianism. Those who have lived their lives attempting to disprove that Utopianism is nothing more the work of science fiction have lost their way. These people of all walks of life such as socialists, Communists, and those others in other political groups. For anyone giving up on the idea of a Utopian society built upon equality and the abolishment of money are in themselves trying to create a world in

D.B. Taylor

their own image and aren't truly worthy of calling themselves socialists.

For the time has arrived and all that is left to do is to free ourselves from the poison of doubt that has been laced within the basis of Socialism and begin a new path in our existence as a species.

From the beginning of time, mankind wasn't meant to live a life in a race against one another. Instead we have set ourselves in a drift in a mindless motion, if we don't set ourselves free from the rat race that has made us all mindless slaves following a dollar on a fishing hook.

For the days leading to a new beginning will be a hard struggle for all those who partake in the fight for freedom. Freedom partaking to the prison that we have allowed ourselves to be held in.

Once the chains have been broken we must form a Workers State that shall exist without borders. With the taking of everything that was once considered the trophies of the wealthily will be nothing more than relics of another time. The majority of the items would be

D.B. Taylor

liquidated and equally divided up and given to the people as a gift, a gift for all the times they went hungry, for when they went cold, for every time they were promised a glimmer of hope but instead received nothing but broken promises.

With this the creation of a society for all workers from all corners of the world will bring about peace and equality.

Within the construction of the Utopian society is to make sure that these four aspects of society are kept in order to preserve the sanctity of society. For if we are to create, to bring life a society, and to keep it thriving for all its citizens. Art, agriculture, education, and the workers. All of these aspects are just a few of what must be met with the highest of respect, as for these four will make the Workers State thrive with vast possibilities to better preserve the image of all who partake in contributing to the society will better themselves and the lives of others.

For this society will not be one led by greed, led by those with materialistic hearts, and exploiting the masses while holding them back from ever achieving their desires.

D.B. Taylor

For the Worker's shall stand tall and Unite under the banner of equality. For it will take the will and spirits of all to stand up and take back their rights, to take back the land, and rights to the resources of the land. With the masses standing up against the one percent the Workers shall take back what's rightfully theirs.

As the days leading up for the all-out revolution, it will take a collective effort from all peoples, at one time shall stand, and take the final death blow to the already crumbling political system and economical system that is lingering alone on life support. Every aspect of life, of society from every nation of the world.

Once the few with the courage take the first stand then more will follow. As the people who are tired of being forced to live by the standards and laws of the one percent and their puppet elected officials. As a people who inhabit this planet, we mustn't let ourselves be imprisoned within the walls that they've built up against us. These people of power who snuck in and force feed us fear all along lining their pockets and turning their backs on the masses.

D.B. Taylor

For once the greed of the few has corrupted all, we see this numerous times within the past, but now it has become that of a faith of the social elite. For those with the means to enslave and hold back the populous as a whole needs to be punished as such. For we've seen their work in the past and which is mentioned within the pages of this book. A method of bathing the world within the pain of the majority, the pain of loss, the pain caused by starvation, the pain of being lied to constantly like that in the way of being a child. Because that is how they see all of us now as, children, uneducated, foolish, mindless, drooling children, and that is why they think they can stand above us and continue to believe that they can continue doing what they think is right for them in the means of profit. While the rest will slowly devolve into what can simply be put into the mind as that of a new Neanderthal species living in squalor along the wayside doing menial labor and waste away like over worked farm animals.

As this is our time to take a stand and forever free ourselves from the chains of oppression.

D.B. Taylor